FOCUS:

Essentials to Build Discipline,

Improve Productivity, and

Eliminate Procrastination to

Achieve Success

Table of Contents

Introduction

In today's busy world, it can often feel like there's too much to be done in too little time. Using time efficiently is imperative to completing tasks on time and leaving yourself enough hours at the end of the day to spend with your family, or doing the things that matter to you. To use your time wisely, however, requires focus, efficiency, and continuous productivity. If you're someone that finds it difficult to keep thinking about the task at hand, or a chronic procrastinator, it can often seem like there are even fewer hours in the day.

Luckily, focus and productivity are skills, and like any skill, they can be learned and practiced. Whether you struggle with procrastination or simply want to find a way to manage your time more efficiently, the information and skills that follow in these chapters will help you to make the most of your work day. The first two chapters focus on ways you can improve your brain's thinking power and set up your physical work space for success. The last three explore multitasking, motivation, and procrastination, looking at ways you can change your habits and develop the discipline to get the most out of your days.

Chapter I: A Healthy Mind

Professional athletes condition their bodies to be in top shape through diet and exercise plans; they understand that staying on top of their physical needs is the best way to achieve consistent high performance. If you work at a desk you may not think physical conditioning is as important, but the truth is it's an important part of your mind's ability to focus. Developing a healthy routine can take enormous discipline, but it will pay off in the long run, ensuring that your physical limitations never get in the way of your ability to achieve your goals.

1: Eat right

Your brain uses about 20% of the energy your body requires while at rest. A balanced diet rich in vitamins, minerals, and protein can drastically improve your productivity and focus. Your nutritional needs as a mental athlete will be different than those of a physical athlete, but balancing your diet around high-nutrition brain foods will help you stay at the top of your game.

To produce neurotransmitters—the cells that carry signals between parts of your brain—you need both vitamin C and tyrosine, an amino acid synthesized within your body from phenylalanine. Phenylalanine is often found in high-protein foods like poultry, milk, and soy, as well as nuts and seeds like almonds or pumpkin seeds. Some botanical fruits—like avocados and bananas—are also high in phenylalanine.

For energy, your brain cells need B vitamins and iron. Leafy greens are some of the best sources of B vitamins. Spinach, mustard greens, and lettuces (romaine and red or green leaf, not iceberg) contain high amounts of B9, while turnip greens and spinach are great sources of B6. Other vegetables high in B vitamins include broccoli, asparagus, and bell peppers. Vitamin B12, meanwhile, is found in fish and liver. Lots of these foods also contain high amounts of iron, letting them serve double-duty on the brain nutrition front—liver, seeds, nuts, and leafy greens are excellent options rich in both iron and B vitamins. Red meat and shellfish can also be excellent sources of dietary iron.

When and how much you eat can also have an impact on your brain's ability to think. Large meals can make you feel tired rather than energized; smaller meals spaced 4-5 hours apart, on the other hand, can serve to give you the energy boost you need to power through your day. If you have trouble getting away from your desk for meals, keep a nutritious snack close at hand, placing an emphasis on proteins and slow-burning carbs. Trail mixes containing almonds or sunflower seeds can make excellent mid-day brain food, though it may be better to make these mixes yourself since most commercial trail mixes are high in sugar, which can make you feel sluggish.

2: Drink plenty of water

Your brain is about 75% water, so keep yourself hydrated throughout the day. Generally, you should try to drink ½-1 ounce of water for each pound you weigh. A 150-pound person, then, would need between 75 and 150 ounces of water daily—around a gallon or more.

Of course, knowing you should drink water and taking time to actually do it can be two very different things. The key is to develop a habit of hydrating regularly throughout the day. Try setting alarms on your phone every few hours reminding you of how many ounces of water you should have consumed by that point in the day. Drinking water with your meals instead of soda can be an easy change. Some people also find it helpful to mark a jug or water bottle using a permanent marker. Make lines on the bottle of how much you should drink by a certain point of the day. Many people live in a state of chronic dehydration, and drinking water regularly will improve not only your mind's functioning but your overall health.

3: Get enough sleep

When you have a lot of obligations, it can be hard to prioritize sleep. A full 6-8 hours a night may seem on the surface like a waste of valuable time, but a well-rested mind will focus better and work more efficiently, ultimately saving yourself time in the long run.

Long-term sleep deprivation is hazardous to your health, but even occasional all-nighters can have a serious effect on your cognitive abilities. Someone who has been awake for 18-20 straight hours has a similar level of impairment to someone with a blood alcohol level of .10%. That's over the legal limit in the United States, meaning someone who's severely sleep deprived is impaired enough to making driving dangerous—not to mention the impact it can have on your critical thinking and decision making skills. When you are sleep deprived, your short-term memory falters, your attention span decreases, and your emotions become more volatile, making you more susceptible to mistakes caused by stress.

If falling asleep at night is difficult for you, there are a few things you can try. Avoiding caffeine and other stimulants after 3 PM will make it easier for your brain to shut down at the end of the night. Avoiding electronic devices for at least an hour before you go to sleep will also help. Whether it's your smart phone or your television, screens stimulate your mind and encourage cognitive activity. The specific kind of light emitted by electronics stimulates the hypothalamus and delays the release of melatonin, a hormone responsible for inducing sleep. Resist the temptation to check your e-mail before bed—whoever you're replying to likely won't be reading your message until the morning, anyway.

4: Exercise

It's no secret that a combination of nutrition and regular exercise is the key to good physical health, but getting your body moving every day can also increase your focus and productivity. Regular exercise prompts the creation of new brain cells in the hippocampus, which is the part of the mind responsible for memory. Aerobic exercise that raises the heart rate immediately increases concentration and focus by stimulating the prefrontal cortex, meaning that if you schedule a session in the gym before you get to work you'll have a better attention span and be better at problem solving for a solid 2-3 hours after your workout ends.

Strenuous exercise also triggers the release of endorphins, chemicals within the brain that boost your mood and increase your ability to prioritize tasks and block out distractions.

Even if you don't have time for a full workout, a little bit of movement can go a long way toward. Instead of reaching for another cup of coffee when you're feeling groggy, try climbing a few flights of stairs or taking a walk around the block—even 15 minutes of activity increases blood flow, which will help your brain get back into the game.

Chapter II: Design Your Space For Success

Changes to your workplace environment can be the easiest way to improve your ability to focus for long spans of time. Unlike changes to your daily routine—which require constant reinforcement and adjustment—a change to your environment is a one and done thing that can increase your concentration without any sustained effort.

Your emphasis should be on minimizing distractions and increasing your comfort. Some of us get more control over our work environments than others. An office with a door will make it much easier to block out interruptions than a cubicle with half-walls; if you own the business or work from a home office, you'll have more power to alter your environment than someone who punches a clock. The truth is, though, that no work environment is absolutely perfect, no matter how much or how little control you have over the specifics. The ability to identify and correct the issues in your working space makes you more adaptable and ultimately more competent, both in work and in life.

1: Good lighting

The human brain reacts differently to artificial lighting than it does to natural sunlight. In a study published by the École Polytechnique Fédérale de Lausanne, subjects were broken into two groups: One was exposed to natural lighting over the course of several work days while the other worked in an environment containing only artificial light. The group deprived of natural light during their day had significantly lower levels of cortisol in their systems at the end of the study. Cortisol is a hormone produced in the adrenal cortex of the human brain. It serves to decrease stress levels and helps metabolize complex sugars, increasing energy levels. In short, those who worked under only artificial light were less able to maintain a level head during crisis situations and were less alert in the later parts of the day. Another study conducted by researchers at Northwestern University of Chicago's Interdepartmental Neuroscience program showed that workers given access to regular natural light reported higher quality of life than their counterparts in terms of physical health and energy levels. They slept an average of 46 more minutes per night, felt more awake throughout the day, and were less likely to suffer from depression, diabetes, and obesity.

Not all of us will be able to work next to a window and reap the benefits of natural light, but there are other ways to get exposure to sunlight throughout your day. When you have a break, leave the office and go outside for at least 15 minutes at a time—even on a cloudy day or in the winter, enough solar radiation is filtering down to earth to give your cortisol levels a little boost. Using a light box at your desk during the day can also simulate the natural light that would come in through a window. Light boxes were designed to treat seasonal affective disorder. They emit safe levels of ultraviolet radiation along with bright white light that mimics sunlight. You don't have to keep the light box on all the time, but keeping one at your desk to turn on when the day is starting to drag can boost your productivity, especially in the winter when the sun often sets before your work day is over.

2: Keep warm (but not too warm)

Cornell University professor Alan Hedge published a study in 2004 linking environmental issues to decreases in worker productivity and the temperature of the working space was found to have a profound impact on employees' ability to focus. Using an insurance company in Florida as their testing ground, the researchers found that low temperatures (68°F or below) caused employees to make 44% more mistakes than those who worked in a comfortable environment. Being cold is a distraction, whether you realize it or not. Your body is using a lot of its energy just to keep itself warm, leaving less for your mind to use on concentration, problem solving, or creativity.

So just crank up the heat and you'll be a super worker, right? Unfortunately, it's not that simple. Being too hot can make you drowsy and less focused. Because your body doesn't have to work as hard to regulate its temperature, your blood pressure drops and you feel more relaxed. That's a wonderful thing when it comes time to settle in for the night, but not as ideal if you're trying to make a deadline.

Professor Hedge determined that the optimal temperature for workers in an office setting is around 77°F (give or take a degree or two). As with the lighting, that's an easy fix to make if you work from a home office or have access to the thermostat, but if you work in a larger building, adjusting the temperature of the entire space may be impossible. In this case, you can turn to portable temperature control. Buy a thermometer to hang in your office or cubicle so you know the score when you settle in. If there's not enough room for a portable space heater, you can find a possible solution at your local pet store in the form of a ceramic heat emitter. Sold in the reptile section, ceramic heat emitters look like opaque black or white light bulbs and are designed to regulate a reptile's night-time temperature without interrupting their circadian rhythm. These "bulbs" will screw into a standard-sized light fixture, though you'll need to buy a ceramic socket—a standard lamp uses plastic that could melt from the heat put off by these devices. You'll find correct fixtures in the reptile section as well, many of which can be easily mounted on the wall of a cubicle or side of a desk. With careful use, a ceramic heat emitter can last up to 10 years, making it a sound investment for a productive future.

3: Comfort and posture

Not only can poor posture and seating affect the long-term health of your back and neck, the muscle strain and tension caused by them can lead to headaches, eyestrain, and poor concentration—after a few hours in this uncomfortable position, you'll be more focused on your discomfort than the task at hand.

While you might have very little control over the padding or support offered by the chairs in your office, you can at least adjust the height to give you the best seating position. To test if your desk and chair are in the correct height ratio, sit in your office chair as you normally would, letting your arms hang at your sides. Bend your elbows 90° so your forearms are exactly perpendicular to your body. This should allow your hands to rest comfortably on the surface of your desk. If they don't, your set-up needs some adjustment. Most computer desks are between 28 and 30 inches high—perfect for someone who's between 5'8" and 5'10" but less ideal if you fall outside that height range. Adjust your office chair up or down until you reach the point your hands rest comfortably on the desk without hunching or straining.

Adjusting your posture could also help give you more energy and a better attention span. The ideal posture in a seated position should put your head in line with your body, with your ears directly over your shoulders. Most people have a tendency to hunch forward while typing or staring at a computer screen, putting far too much strain on your neck and back. For each inch your head is too far forward it adds ten extra pounds of pressure to your neck—and if you hold that position throughout an 8-hour work day, it's a recipe for aches and potential joint damage. Just like with the improper desk height, this leads to discomfort and distraction that can break your focus. The best way to assess your posture is to sit in front of a mirror. Your shoulders should slope slightly downward—if they're raised, that means you're carrying a lot of tension in your upper back. Raise them up intentionally for a second or two then relax completely; after that, make sure your chin is level and your head is perfectly in line with your neck. Once you've found this posture, hold it for a few seconds while looking at yourself in the mirror, paying special attention to how this posture feels. Check in on your posture throughout the day when you start to feel sore, anxious, or distracted. Bad posture is an unconscious habit that can take a lot of discipline to un-learn, but correcting bad posture will allow you to work longer without distraction or pain.

4: The right kind of background noise

Anyone who's tried reading a book in a public space knows that too much noise can be distracting, but it may surprise you to learn that too little noise can have an equally adverse effect on your productivity. Too much noise puts stress on your nervous system by increasing your pulse rate and blood pressure. Your mind is actively working to block out the extra noise, which can be both physically and mentally exhausting, making you expend more energy to complete the same tasks and diminishing your ability to focus.

Too little noise leads to a different kind of distraction because of the relative decibel level. The best way to think about this is by using your television as an example. The volume level you set your TV set to during the day seems uncomfortably loud if you're watching it late at night. This isn't because the television itself is louder; rather, the background noise of the world outside is diminished, making the television seem louder in comparison. Translated to a workplace environment, a completely silent office means that every little sound—whether it's a conversation in the breakroom or a ringing phone—is a drastic contrast to the baseline decibel level. Your ear picks up on this sound and your concentration is broken.

The best way to combat this depends on your personal situation. Some people find that soft music helps to aid concentration. If you're working with words—like reading e-mails or writing a report—instrumental music will be ideal. Lyrics in songs are processed in the same verbal centers of the brain that handle other linguistic tasks and may interfere with your thought processes. Using headphones to play this music can be especially helpful, as the headphones themselves provide another level of protection from potentially distracting sounds (and, as a bonus, provide a nice visual cue to your colleagues that you're in work mode and prefer not to be disturbed). Investing in a good pair of noise-cancelling headphones can take your distraction-free set-up to the next level.

For some people, even instrumental music can be a distraction. If this is the case for you, consider using a white noise app or buying a looping track of nature sound effects, like rainfall or ocean waves. Not only will these provide a constant decibel that makes other workplace noises less jarring, they have a calming effect on your neurons, allowing your brain to stay

focused for longer.

Chapter III: The Dangers of Multitasking

The ability to multitask is regarded necessary skill in today's busy, modern world—and with most of us having more to do than there are hours in the day, it's easy to understand why. On the surface, multitasking seems like an opportunity to accomplish two tasks in the time it would normally take to accomplish one. As is so often the case, however, the reality of the situation is far more complicated. While the modern world considers multitasking a valued skill, it actually contributes to increased workplace stress and may be damaging your focus, productivity, and efficiency more than you realize.

As early as 2001, studies emerged on the dangers and damages of multitasking. An article published in the *Journal of Experimental Psychology: Human Perception and Performance* entitled "Executive

Control of Cognitive Processes in Task Switching"
showed that subjects lost time switching from one
task to another compared to completing individual
tasks in a linear fashion. The more complex the task,
the greater the time lost—as much as 40%, the study
found. More recently, a 2010 article entitled "Being of
Two Minds: Switching Mindsets Exhausts Self-
Regulatory Resources" showed that multitasking not
only makes you less efficient at executing the tasks at
hand, it also causes mental exhaustion that inhibited
subjects' ability to perform follow-up tasks and
negatively affected their decision making skills and
short term memory. In other words, not only does
multitasking decrease your workplace efficiency, it
makes it harder to focus in the long-term. Studies
done on high school and college students dating back
as far as 1993 also demonstrated a lower retention
rate among those who multitasked while studying.

They performed worse on exams and were less able to recall the information they had supposedly learned even a short time after reviewing their notes.

The truth is, the human brain is not capable of multitasking, in the sense of working on two tasks simultaneously. When you multitask, your brain is actually switching its focus from one task to another. The more familiar the task, the less your brain has to work to switch; the more complex the task, the more likely you are to lose focus and make potentially detrimental mistakes.

This may seem like dire news. The ability to juggle two tasks at once has become something of a prerequisite for most high-level employment—not to mention the multitasking involved in balancing family life with work life. Smart phones and other electronic devices mean many of us are trying to multitask almost constantly without ever realizing that we're doing it.

Luckily, by making some simple changes to your daily routine you can limit the amount of task switching your brain does every day. While these changes require some discipline to initially implement, the improvement you'll see in your ability to focus makes them well worth the effort.

1: Make a schedule—and keep to it

Your mind is at its most efficient when it can work for an extended period of time on tasks involving the same mindset. One of the most mentally taxing mindsets is the decision making process—in other words, deciding what task to work on next can be one of the biggest focus breakers. Take 5-10 minutes either the night before or first thing in the morning to outline your tasks for the day, considering the complexity of the various things you have to do and the basic mindset you'll need to be in while doing them. Alternate complex tasks with more simple ones to let your brain rest between intense thinking sessions. Separating your day into sections based on the type of task makes it do less switching and lose less time.

Objective tasks that require little cognitive effort—like basic math, checking mail, or data entry—are the least complex and the easiest for your mind to switch into or between. Subjective tasks—decision making, creative problem solving, or analysis and synthesis of data—involve more areas of your brain at once and will take longer to get back into once you're interrupted. If you know there's a certain time of day you're likely to be interrupted, schedule simpler tasks during that time, reserving larger blocks of uninterrupted time for the tasks that require more discipline and energy. While some things are clearly more complex, this can also be a personal decision. If you feel more comfortable with words than with numbers, tasks involving lots of numbers will be more taxing for you; reserve the most uninterrupted time to complete these items, saving the relatively easier tasks for more hectic times of day.

It can also help to do the most complex and difficult tasks early in the day before your mind has a chance to tire, though that isn't necessarily the case for everyone. If you know your brain is more efficient in the afternoon than first thing in the morning, don't try to force yourself into an arbitrary system. Schedule complex tasks for your own brain's most efficient time for more consistent success. You may also find it harder to avoid interruptions earlier in the morning because of calls, e-mails, or the schedules of your colleagues. Even if morning is your most efficient time, frequent interruptions will negate your brain's normal high functioning during this time. If you can't eliminate the interruptions, it may be better to tailor your schedule around them.

2: Designate communication times

This was touched on above but deserves a special notice because of how damaging it can be to your long-term ability to focus. In our totally connected modern world, you are constantly at the whim of interruptions from the outside world if you don't take specific steps to prevent them. Whether it's a text message, an e-mail, or a phone call, incoming communication draws you instantly away from whatever task you're working on—and if that's a complex task, it could take up to 15 minutes just to get back into the flow, not even considering the time spent replying to the message. Silence alerts from your inbox on both your phone and computer when you're working on other things and designate 3-4 times throughout the day that are specifically reserved for communications. If you work in an office with colleagues who are prone to interrupting you, tell them when your "complex work time" is and ask them not to disturb you. If your colleagues have trouble respecting time boundaries, try putting on a Bluetooth headset; most people won't disturb you if they think you're on the phone.

3: Take daily screen breaks

Looking at various screens throughout the day can send your mind into information overload. Obviously this includes your phone and computer, but even staring at the television during your relaxation time can wear out your brain more than you may think: Commercials interrupt programs in much the same way an e-mail can interrupt your thinking time and having the TV on in the background while doing other tasks is still a form of multitasking. Even if you can't remove the interruptions during your day, scheduling yourself a couple hours of screen-free time can give your brain an opportunity to recharge. Try to avoid all screens for an hour before going to sleep, and again for the first hour in the morning. Even if you're working during this time—for example, writing out your day's schedule by hand—the limiting of tasks and interruptions will mean less work for your brain.

Chapter IV: What's My Motivation?

Motivation to accomplish tasks and goals can be divided into two groups: Extrinsic motivation, which comes from an outside source, and intrinsic motivation, which comes from within. An example of extrinsic motivation would be meeting a deadline for a project, or a bonus offered by your company. Intrinsic motivation can work towards these rewards, but the rewards themselves aren't the main motivator; your main reason for working toward the goal is a sense of personal fulfillment. Both intrinsic and extrinsic motivation can be at play at the same time. As an example, think of a professional hockey goaltender training in the off-season. His extrinsic motivations to improve his conditioning are the expectations of his teammates, coaches, and fans that he will lead the team to victory; on a more practical level, his extrinsic motivation may be the paycheck he is receiving from the team in exchange for playing at his best. His intrinsic motivation could be as simple as the joy he gets from playing hockey, or something more goal-oriented, like his personal desire to win a Stanley Cup. If the goaltender was traded to another team, the source of his extrinsic motivations would change, but the intrinsic motivation will remain with him regardless of where he plays.

Both extrinsic and intrinsic motivation can be successful at fueling people toward accomplishing a task, but intrinsic motivation is the stronger of the two, and someone who is only fueled by extrinsic motivation is less likely to succeed in the long-term. People who rely on exclusively extrinsic motivation rely on external factors to validate their worth—they can see their own value only when someone else has acknowledged it. This constant need for external validation means they will feel more pressure, stress, and anxiety. This often leads to depression when external approval isn't available. An extrinsically motivated person is also less likely to try again after a failure and has limited avenues for self-improvement. Say the goaltender from the above example has a few bad games and is pulled in favor of his back-up. If he relies exclusively on extrinsic motivation, this becomes a crushing failure that can rob him of his confidence and prevent him from returning to his usual high level of play; what would have been validation had he won those games becomes pressure instead, and his sense of self-worth and accomplishment are diminished. On the other hand, if the goaltender is intrinsically motivated, he can see that this particular slump is merely a set-back and will be better able to retain his sense of self-worth based on his long-term personal progress. Intrinsically motivated people are better at handling constructive criticism and can recover from failures because their perceived self-worth doesn't hinge on accomplishment.

Even the most successful and illustrious career will have occasional low points. Cultivating your own intrinsic motivation is important to maintaining productivity and not getting derailed by occasional set-backs. Even the most motivated person, however, will occasionally need boosts from the outside world to remind them of their path and goals. Maintaining a balance between intrinsic and extrinsic motivation is key to cultivating the discipline required for long-term success, and while you don't have much control over the extrinsic motivation you're given, you can develop a greater sense of intrinsic motivation to improve your productivity.

1: Give yourself rewards

One extrinsic motivator you can establish for yourself is to give yourself rewards when you accomplish a task or goal. This can be as small as a favorite candy bar or as big as a new car, but always be sure to match the size of the reward to the size of the goal—for example, achieving a sales quota for the week could earn you a night out at the movies, but if that's your reward for meeting a yearly sales quota, it will seem a little cheap; something more expansive, like a week-long cruise, may be in order. Make the reward concrete instead of abstract. Write your goal on a piece of paper along with the reward you'll get when you complete it. For long-term goals, put this piece of paper up on your desk where you can see it, to remind yourself of the good things coming when you finish your task. It's also important to keep your expectations of yourself realistic. If you try to do a week's worth of work in a day, you'll set yourself up for failure and never receive the designated reward, which will have the opposite effect you're looking for, making you feel bitter and worthless.

2: Keep your bigger goals in mind

If you're having trouble staying focused on the task at hand, figure out how it fits into your ultimate life goals. Let's say, for example, that your goal is to retire at age 65, and the task is writing a quarterly budget for your company. On the surface, the two may seem unrelated, but if you think about it more carefully you'll see they're directly related. Doing good work on the budget and turning it in before the deadline will prove you to be a dependable and good worker; a history of dependable high-quality work will put you in a better position to request a raise or a promotion; a higher wage will allow you to put more money into your retirement fund. In a way, it's like playing that old movie game "six degrees of Kevin Bacon." The links are always there—you just have to find them. Once you've figured out how the task connects into your larger goal, think about that goal, and not just in the abstract. Close your eyes for a moment and picture yourself having achieved it. In the case of retirement, perhaps you will picture yourself spending time doing a favorite hobby, or visiting a place you've always wanted to go. Imagine your perfect scenario, and don't be afraid to dream big—remember that the key here is to make yourself excited to work. By connecting seemingly menial tasks into the larger picture, you take something you're working on for someone else and make it an individual task— something you're working on to help yourself. This can also work to amplify the motivation already provided externally. If higher sales will earn you a bonus, think about exactly what you plan to do with that bonus, whether it's take your family on a vacation or finally pay off a credit card. Think about how good you'll feel when you're spending that bonus any time your productivity begins to flag.

People who are trying to lose weight are often advised to put a picture of their ideal body on the fridge so they can see it and remember their bigger goal when they're tempted to over-indulge. When you're looking at a reminder of your ultimate goals, it's easier to maintain your focus when facing the hardships and tedium of the road to success. You can use a similar tactic at your desk. In the retirement example above, find an image or an object that can remind you of what you'll do once you have time—a postcard from your ideal vacation spot, perhaps, or a baseball to remind yourself you'll be able to take your grandchildren to games. Put it somewhere you can see it easily while you're working. When you feel your mind wandering and your focus waning, that object or image can serve as a reminder of what you can achieve if you maintain your productivity.

3: Regain your joy

A lot of people get into a field they truly enjoy and then find their enjoyment of it fading as the work becomes routine. This is a common effect of a task shifting from intrinsic to extrinsic motivation, and can happen even in jobs you may think are immune to the daily grind. A professional pianist who used to practice for hours on end without complaint may find it suddenly torturous after securing a job with a local symphony. It's not caused by fatigue, though that's what it may seem like on the surface. When the pianist played for free, it was purely intrinsic motivation—they were doing it out of love, and so had no reason not to enjoy it. Once they started getting paid to do it, however, it became an extrinsically motivated task—this is a job that they're doing for money. The same task done for different motivations takes on an entirely different flavor.

Changing the motivation back to an intrinsic one in your mind can help you to regain the passion—or at least the interest—that drew you to this field in the first place. Take a moment to write down everything you enjoy about the field you work in. Focus on the field and your own personal enjoyment, not your specific job; things like "it pays well" are still extrinsic motivations. Even if you're in a field that's not traditionally very glamorous, there is something that either drew you to the job or made you stay that gives you great satisfaction. If you're a financial advisor, maybe it's helping people realize their dreams, or the excitement of following the changes in the stock market. No one else is going to see this, so let yourself genuinely geek out about your job. If you're an accountant because you really enjoy playing with numbers, embrace that; if you're a car salesman because you love the smell of a leather interior, don't be afraid to admit it. Finding the joy in the small, every day parts of your job will keep you focused so you can complete the larger, more exciting tasks.

Chapter V: Eliminating Procrastination

It is a common misconception that procrastination is caused by inherent laziness. Procrastination is a complex issue that is more often a symptom of avoidance, sensory overload, or indecision.

Sometimes, your brain knows that you have X number of tasks to complete, and because it can't decide which one is best to start with, the end result is not working on any of them at all. At other times, there are simply too many options, and your brain freezes because it's overwhelmed. Fear and anxiety can also play huge roles in a person's tendency to chronically procrastinate. The ultimate cure for procrastination is working smarter, not working harder.

One thing that it's important to keep in mind is that different people procrastinate for different reasons. According to Dr. Joseph Ferrari, professor of psychology at De Paul University, there are three main types of chronic procrastinators. Arousal-type procrastinators wait until the last minute because they crave the excitement of working down to the wire. This is the type of procrastinator who's most likely to say they "work best under pressure." Avoidance-type procrastinators are paralyzed by their fear of failure. They are often very concerned with the opinions of others, to the point they'd rather do no work at all and appear lazy than turn in work that's judged unworthy. Finally, decisional procrastinators are unable to choose a course of action and, because of that, get stuck circling the problem without ever doing anything about it.

Granted, not everyone is a chronic procrastinator. Many people who occasionally procrastinate are perfectly capable of handling most of the tasks they're given on a reasonable schedule. Looking at these habits of chronic procrastinators, though, can help you to overcome those moments that you do put things off. Consider carefully and honestly why you can't bring yourself to work on the task at hand. Where do you fit in Dr. Ferrari's procrastination types? Are you unsure of where to start? Do you lack confidence in your ability to complete the task required? Sometimes even just thinking about a project and why it's giving you trouble can be enough to end the procrastination. If not, there are some other things you can try to get the productive juices flowing.

1: Small tasks build toward big goals

This technique can be helpful for procrastinators of all stripes, and is especially useful when working on long and complex projects. Write down the end goal of the task that you're procrastinating at the top of a piece of paper, then start breaking it down into smaller and smaller pieces in a branching fashion until you've gotten to a level that feels manageable. Let's say, for example, that the task at hand is to put together a presentation. The second-level tasks for this project might be design a Power Point and prepare your speech. The Power Point presentation could be further divided into writing the text, preparing the graphics, making the slide transitions, and so on, until something catches your eye that you feel comfortable working on.

The main advantage of breaking down a larger task into its component parts is that it can make the entire project feel less overwhelming. It also lets you set secondary deadlines for yourself along the way, especially helpful if you know you have a tendency to put off working on larger tasks until the last minute. By sorting out the tasks, you may also find components of the project that can complement each other. In the example above, let's say you start with writing the text for your Power Point. That text can then serve as the foundation for preparing what you're going to say along with the presentation. Spotting these moments of convergence makes the entire project less daunting, while the secondary deadlines let you feel like you're accomplishing things along the way and can diminish the fear of failure in avoidance-type procrastination.

2: Prioritizing

Ordering and prioritizing the tasks at hand can be especially helpful in cases of procrastination fueled by indecision. When you have a lot on your plate, deciding what is most important or time-sensitive can help you determine which task to tackle first. Start by making a list of all the assignments, tasks, and projects you need to get done. Rank them initially from first to last in order of which you perceive to be the most important. Once you've done this, write down the deadline beside the task, along with a realistic estimate of how long it's going to take you to complete. If there's no definite deadline, assign yourself one—you're more likely to pay attention to a task that's on a ticking clock than one with a nebulous completion date. Now rank the tasks again, this time on the basis of timeliness.

The reason you want to approach this from both the deadline and the importance standpoint is that it lets you see, at a glance, where your deadlines and your priorities converge. A task that's due next week will need to get your attention now, even if you don't consider it to be so important; a task that's very important and time consuming, even though it's not due for three months, will warrant occasional attention in between other more time-sensitive assignments to prevent it from becoming a last-minute race to the end. Sketch out a rough plan of attack for all your projects, then check back to your list and revise it as you turn in projects or receive new assignments.

3: Take your project on a first date

Sometimes the hardest part of focusing on a task is knowing where to start. When this is the case, dedicating quality time to brainstorming or working on the task at hand is crucial. It's best if you can do this the analog way, using pen and paper; if your line of work demands the use of technology, turn off your Wi-Fi so you're not tempted to waste time checking your e-mail or browsing the internet. Also turn off or silence your phone and have the discipline not to check it. Unless your work demands you be in a specific office or studio space, it's best if you can go to a neutral territory that's neither in your home or your office. A coffee shop or restaurant can be perfect for this, or a public park or garden if the weather allows it. The purpose of this is two-fold. One, the change of scenery breaks you out of your normal routines and may let you approach the issue from a different angle. Two, it prevents your colleagues or family from inadvertently breaking your focus. It can also give the process an inherent reward. Let yourself get that salted caramel mocha you've been craving, or go to that little bistro you've been meaning to visit, if it will give you the motivation you need to sit down and hash out the work you've been avoiding. If you are especially sensitive to background noise, you can bring a pair of headphones and listen to music as you work; you may find, however, that the background volume in your average cafe or park is just enough white noise to let you concentrate in peace.

Give your project at least an hour; two or three is better, if you have the time for it. Treat the project like it's an attractive person, or an old friend—someone you would look forward to sharing time with. Schedule this brainstorming session in your planner and don't let yourself cancel the date unless there's an actual emergency. If you do have to cancel it, re-schedule the date immediately. Don't have any expectations in mind in terms of tangible results or accomplishments. Especially if your procrastination is fueled by anxiety or a fear of failure, a pre-conceived expectation of results will likely only serve to make you tense up and freeze. The goal is to remove yourself from your typical constraints, letting your mind feel out the project without stress or distraction.

4: Hold yourself accountable

You often hear about people who were straight-A students through school that have trouble adjusting to the working world. There are of course a multitude of things that can cause this, but one main thing is that, in school, there is a teacher assigning tasks, setting due dates, and giving out grades to tell you how well you've done. While a performance review is something like a grade, figuring out what tasks to do and when can often be at your discretion in the workplace. If you're writing a report in a college class, you'll have separate due dates for the outline, the first draft, and so on, all the way through to the finished project. In a workplace environment, you're expected to manage your own time through the process; most people outside of school care only about your results. If you find you're having trouble starting and finishing tasks on time, buy a notebook and designate it your work journal. Start each day writing down what you plan to accomplish, then jot down brief notes as you go through your day—when you start tasks, when you finish them, and any particular challenges or issues that arose as you were working. Review your work journal once a week. What percentage of your "to-do list" have you been accomplishing in the average day? Which tasks are taking longer than others? Are there any consistent issues that came up during your work? Workshop and review your process as if it were completed by a student, and you are the teacher. If this were a stranger's work journal, what critiques would you make of it?

A work journal lets you see which tasks you've been avoiding before they fall completely off your radar. It also lets you evaluate your work process and make the most efficient use of your day. If you're working steadily and still consistently not completing your tasks, you may be over-estimating what is a realistic

amount of work to accomplish in a day; that, more
than procrastination, could be the source of your
stress and missed deadlines.

Conclusion

I hope you were able to gain a clear understanding of how to improve your focus and the different steps that you can take to achieve your full potential achieve success.

It is now up to you to take the necessary action to change your habits and improve your focus. Don't worry, for it is never too late to enjoy true intelligence and happiness because anyone can learn something new at any age. What matters is you believe in yourself.

www.ingramcontent.com/pod-product-compliance
Lightning Source LLC
Chambersburg PA
CBHW070404190526
45169CB00003B/1099